MY VERY OWN SUKKOT BOOK

by
Judyth Robbins Saypol
Madeline Wikler

KAR-BEN COPIES, INC.   ROCKVILLE, MARYLAND

Library of Congress Cataloging in Publication Data

Saypol, Judyth R.
  My very own Sukkot book.

  Cover title: My very own Sukkot.
  Summary: Explains the significance of Sukkot, an autumn holiday celebrating the harvest. Includes stories, songs, prayers, and a home service.
  1. Sukkoth—Juvenile Literature. [1. Sukkoth. 2. Judaism—Customs and practices. 3. Fasts and feasts—Judaism] I. Wikler, Madeline, 1943-   . II. Title. III. Title: My very own Sukkot.
  BM695.S8S28   1983   296.4'33   83-26738
  ISBN 0-930494-09-1 (pbk.)

Second Printing, 1983

Copyright © 1980 by KAR-BEN Copies, Inc. All rights reserved. No portion of this book may be reproduced without the written permission of the publisher.

Published by KAR-BEN Copies, Inc., Rockville, MD 20852
Printed in the United States of America.

CONTENTS

	PAGES
Sukkot in History	5-11
The Sukkah	12-13
Lulav and Etrog	14-17
Sukkot Today	18-21
Shemini Atzeret	22
Home Service	23-30
Music	31-37
Building and Decorating a Sukkah	38-39

For everything there is a season.
For everything there is a time.

A time to weep and a time to laugh.
A time to keep silent and a time to speak.
A time to plant and a time to harvest.

Summer is over. The farmers have gathered the crops from the fields. Leaves are changing color and falling from the trees. Autumn rains are here. The days are getting shorter.

The time of Sukkot has come.
Sukkot celebrates the season of the harvest.

Sukkot is a festival with many names and many meanings. The holiday is called Chag HaSukkot, the festival of booths. The Torah tells us —

> The fifteenth day of the seventh month (Tishri) shall be a festival.

> You shall live in booths for seven days, so you may remember that the Jewish people lived in booths when they were freed from slavery in Egypt.

Sukkot is a holiday when we remember the history of the Jewish people.

The holiday is also called Chag HaAsif, the festival of the harvest. The Torah tells us —

> When you have gathered in the harvest crops at the end of the year, you shall celebrate. You shall take the branches and fruit of beautiful trees, and you shall rejoice.

Sukkot is a celebration of nature. The lulav and etrog stand for the harvest crops that provide our food.

Sukkot is also called Zeman Simchatenu, the season of gladness. The Torah tells us to be happy on Sukkot.

A HOLIDAY OF HISTORY

Jewish people all over the world share a long history. Our holidays help us to remember important times in this history.

On Pesach we retell the story of how we were slaves in Egypt.

On Shavuot we remember when Moses and the Jewish people received the Torah.

Sukkot reminds us that after the Jewish people left Egypt, they wandered in the desert for 40 years. They were often tired and hungry. They built huts (sukkot) for shade and rest. The huts were not very big or comfortable. But the people shared a dream.

> They would be free in their own land...
> A land with rivers and trees and fruit...
> A land where they could build homes to protect them.

Building a sukkah reminds us of our history.

A HOLIDAY OF NATURE

Long ago, the Jewish people were shepherds and farmers. During the growing season, they went out to work in the fields, and came home to their villages at night.

But during the harvest, there was no time for the farmers to return to their villages. The fruits and vegetables were ripe and would spoil if not picked quickly. So the farmers built huts in the fields for shelter and rest.

When the harvest was finished, the farmers celebrated. They were thankful that they had enough food for the long winter.

Building a sukkah is a celebration of nature.

THE SEASON OF GLADNESS

Long ago, Jews from all over the world travelled to Jerusalem to celebrate holidays at the Holy Temple. The travellers were called pilgrims, and their journey was called a pilgrimage. Sukkot was a favorite time for such a trip, because the work of the harvest was over.

Thousands of Jews came. Rich Jews drove chariots, others rode donkeys and camels. Most travelled on foot. They spoke many languages and had different customs, but they were one Jewish people.

The streets were decorated with fruits and branches. There were parades and dances, sacrifices and feasts.

The pilgrims needed shelter, so they built sukkot in courtyards and on rooftops.

Building a sukkah reminds us of the pilgrimage to Jerusalem.

THE WATER-DRAWING CEREMONY

The rabbis said that on Sukkot, God decides how much rain will fall during the coming year. In Israel, the summer is completely dry. Fall and winter rains prepare the earth for spring planting. If there is no rain, there will be no crops, and people will be hungry.

During the Sukkot celebration at the Holy Temple a special rain ceremony was held. People marched to a nearby spring, drew water in golden pitchers, and poured it on the Temple altar. Golden lamps were lit in the Temple courtyard, the shofar was blown, and the people sang and danced all night to the music of trumpets, harps, and cymbals.

SUKKAH

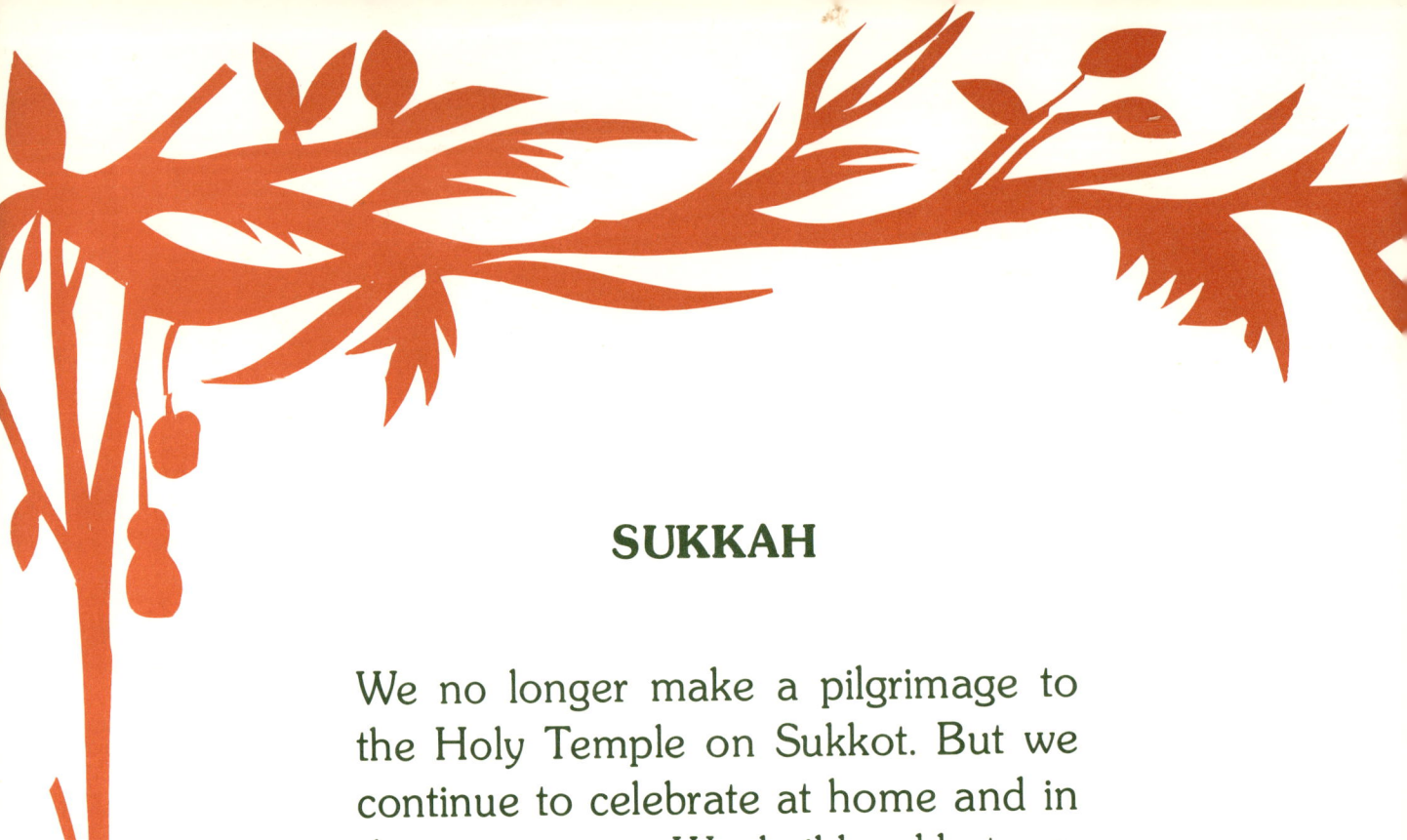

We no longer make a pilgrimage to the Holy Temple on Sukkot. But we continue to celebrate at home and in the synagogue. We build sukkot, rejoice with lulav and etrog, and pray for life-giving rain.

On Sukkot we leave our comfortable homes and find shelter under leaves and branches.

The most important part of the sukkah is the roof (schach). It must be made from things that grow. It must be open to the light of the sun, moon, and stars.

The sukkah reminds us of:

- shelters the Jewish people built in the desert
- harvest huts the Israelite farmers built in the fields
- huts the Jewish pilgrims built in Jerusalem on Sukkot

The sukkah is not strong. It shakes in the wind and rain.

It reminds us that even though we live in sturdy homes, not all families live in peace, comfort, and safety.

Building a sukkah is a mitzvah.

LULAV AND ETROG

The Torah tells us that on Sukkot, we shall take the branches and fruit of beautiful trees, and rejoice.

We fulfill this mitzvah by holding four crops — called "arba'at haminim" — and reciting a blessing over them during the holiday.

These are the crops we use:

Lulav — the branch of a palm tree bound with:
    Hadasim — three boughs of a leafy myrtle tree
    Aravot — two branches of a willow tree
    Etrog — the fruit of a citron tree

Each of the crops in the lulav and etrog is different:

> The etrog is both sweet-smelling and tasty.
>
> Dates, the fruit of the lulav, have taste but no smell.
>
> Hadasim (myrtle branches) have smell but no taste.
>
> Aravot (willows) have neither taste nor smell.

The lulav and etrog together stand for many things:

- the plentiful crops in the land of Israel
- the harvest of the ancient farmers
- the harvest we enjoy today
- our need for rain

Some say that together these crops stand for all people — the wise and the foolish, the kind and the selfish, the young and the old.

Others say that the lulav and etrog are like parts of our bodies:

> The tall, stately lulav is our backbone.
>
> The almond-shaped hadasim are our eyes.
>
> The slender aravot leaves are our lips.
>
> The etrog is our heart.

Aravot (willows) and hadasim (myrtles) grow in many lands, but the lulav and etrog need warm climates. When our grandparents and great-grandparents lived in the villages of Eastern Europe, they had to get their lulav and etrog from Israel or another warm country. Most families could not afford to buy their own and had to share. Children would carry the lulav and etrog from house to house each morning so that every family could recite the blessings. When Sukkot was over, they would make the rounds again to receive their payment.

SUKKOT AT HOME

There are many ways to celebrate Sukkot at home. If we build a sukkah, we can eat meals and snacks there. It is also a nice place to read and study, and, if the weather is nice, we can even sleep there. Some people who don't build sukkot decorate their homes with fruit and branches. Each morning, except on Shabbat, we bless the lulav and etrog in the sukkah.

Part of the joy of Sukkot is to celebrate with friends and family. It is a custom to invite Biblical heroes to join us in the Sukkah. This custom is called "ushpizin," which means guests. We invite Abraham, Isaac, Jacob, Joseph, Moses, Aaron and David. You can decorate your sukkah with their names, or set aside a chair for them. Some families read or tell stories about these heroes during holiday meals.

SUKKOT IN THE SYNAGOGUE

The synagogue, which is a quiet, serious place on Rosh Hashanah and Yom Kippur, becomes festive on Sukkot. During Hallel, special prayers of praise to God, we wave our lulav and etrog. After we read from the Torah, there is a parade. The rabbi, cantor, and congregation march around the bimah and down the aisles carrying the lulav and etrog. After services, we gather in the synagogue sukkah for kiddush and refreshments.

SUKKOT AND THANKSGIVING

Thanksgiving and Sukkot have much in common. This is not surprising. The Bible was a very important book for the early American settlers. They named their children after Biblical heroes, such as Benjamin, Joshua, Ruth, and Rachel, and gave Biblical names like Canaan, Sinai, and Jordan to their towns and cities.

The pilgrims compared their voyage to America to the Exodus from Egypt. The Atlantic Ocean was their Red Sea, and America was their Promised Land. In 1621, when the Pilgrims gathered to give thanks for a good harvest after their first hard year in the New World, they were reminded of the Biblical festival of Sukkot, and created a harvest festival of their own.

SUKKOT IN ISRAEL TODAY

Today, many Israelis live on kibbutzim, and farming is one of Israel's most important industries. Many kibbutzim build huge sukkot, large enough for all of their members to eat in. They are decorated with fruits and vegetables grown and harvested on the kibbutz.

The kibbutzim depend on rain for their crops, and many hold special ceremonies, much like the water-drawing ceremony at the Holy Temple. They gather at a nearby spring and dance and sing about "mayim", water.

וּשְׁאַבְתֶּם מַיִם בְּשָׂשׂוֹן מִמַּעַיְנֵי הַיְשׁוּעָה.

Ushavtem mayim b'sasson mima'anei hayeshuah.

Joyfully shall you draw water from the fountains of salvation.

SHEMINI ATZERET

A king once arranged a great feast and invited many people to his palace. After they had spent many happy days together, the guests prepared to leave. The king said to them, "Please stay with me one more day. It is hard for me to say good-bye."

So it is with Sukkot. It is a happy week, and we would like it to last just one day longer. Shemini Atzeret, the Eighth Day of Gathering, is the closing holiday which follows Sukkot. In the synagogue there are Yizkor prayers to honor those who have died. After the Torah is read, we recite a beautiful prayer for rain:

Dear God, who causes the wind to blow and the rain to fall,
Bring us the blessing of gentle showers.
Crown the valleys with green fruits.
Cool the dried and heated earth with life-giving rain.

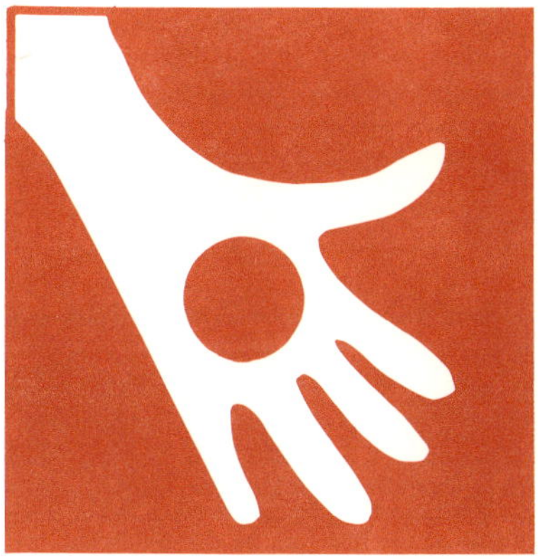

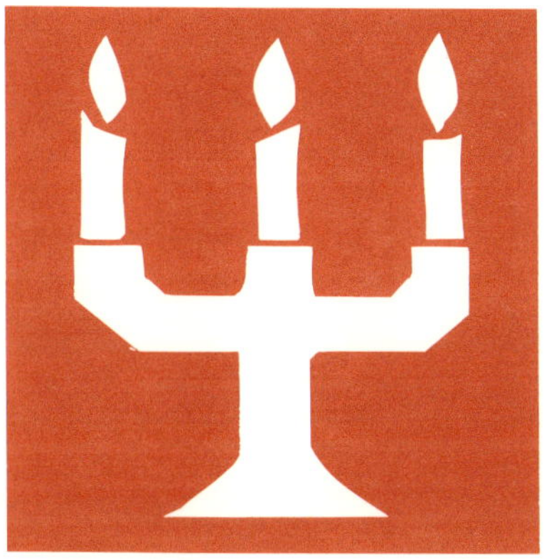

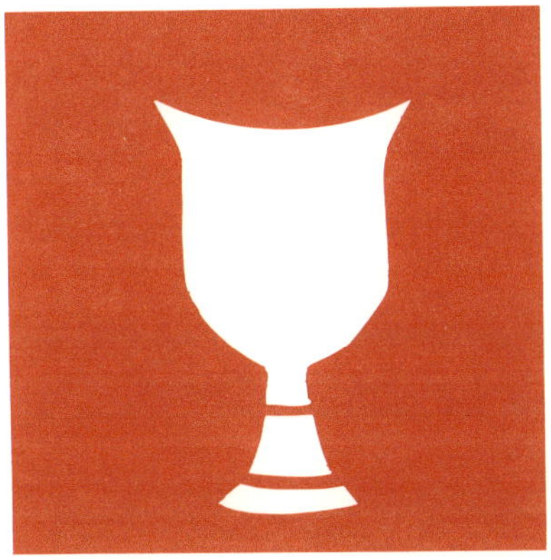

TZEDAKAH

Tzedakah was an important mitzvah for Jewish farmers, especially at Sukkot time.

The Torah commands the farmers to share their harvest. They were required to leave a small portion of their crops unpicked, so the poor might gather them for food. They had to set aside a tithe (a tenth) of their grain, oil, wine, and livestock to share with others. A portion of this tithe was given to the Holy Temple to feed the priests and levites, and a portion was used to feed the needy. When the Jewish pilgrims came to Jerusalem, they brought additional gifts, some of which were sold to raise money for the Temple.

Today, we show our concern for the poor, and our support for our synagogues and Jewish organizations by giving money for tzedakah. Some families and schools also collect food to share with needy persons during Sukkot.

HADLAKAT NEROT
BLESSING OVER THE CANDLES

We welcome Sukkot with the lighting of the candles.

בָּרוּךְ אַתָּה יְיָ, אֱלֹהֵינוּ מֶלֶךְ הָעוֹלָם, אֲשֶׁר קִדְּשָׁנוּ בְּמִצְוֹתָיו, וְצִוָּנוּ לְהַדְלִיק נֵר שֶׁל יוֹם טוֹב.

Baruch atah adonai eloheinu melech ha'olam asher kideshanu b'mitzvotav v'tzivanu l'hadlik ner shel yom tov.

Thank you, God, for bringing our family together to celebrate Sukkot and for the mitzvah of lighting the candles. As the glow of the moon and stars brings light to our Sukkah, so may these candles shine upon us in joy and in peace.

KIDDUSH

BLESSING OVER THE WINE

The Kiddush proclaims the holiness of Sukkot. We sing blessings over the cup of wine in honor of the Festival of the Harvest.

בָּרוּךְ אַתָּה יְיָ, אֱלֹהֵינוּ מֶלֶךְ הָעוֹלָם,

בּוֹרֵא פְּרִי הַגָּפֶן.

Baruch atah adonai eloheinu melech haolam borei pri hagafen.

Thank you, God, for the harvest of the vineyards, from which wine is made for our Sukkot celebration.

Thank you, God, for this season of gladness. We remember our people's history, and rejoice in the bounty of the earth.

BLESSINGS IN THE SUKKAH

We have worked to build and decorate our sukkah. We gather now to enjoy our work, and to fulfill the mitzvah of eating in the Sukkah.

בָּרוּךְ אַתָּה יְיָ, אֱלֹהֵינוּ מֶלֶךְ הָעוֹלָם, אֲשֶׁר קִדְּשָׁנוּ בְּמִצְוֹתָיו, וְצִוָּנוּ לֵישֵׁב בַּסֻּכָּה.

Baruch atah adonai eloheinu melech haolam asher kideshanu b'mitzvotav v'tzivanu leshev basukkah.

Thank you, God, for the festival we enjoy while we dwell in the sukkah.

בָּרוּךְ אַתָּה יְיָ, אֱלֹהֵינוּ מֶלֶךְ הָעוֹלָם, שֶׁהֶחֱיָנוּ וְקִיְּמָנוּ וְהִגִּיעָנוּ לַזְּמַן הַזֶּה.

Baruch atah adonai eloheinu melech haolam shehecheyanu, v'kiyemanu, v'higianu laz'man hazeh.
(This blessing is recited on the first two nights only.)

Thank you, God, for bringing our family and friends together in this season of our gladness.

HAMOTZI

BLESSING OVER THE CHALLAH

As we enjoy our challah, we are grateful for the abundance of the harvest.

בָּרוּךְ אַתָּה יְיָ, אֱלֹהֵינוּ מֶלֶךְ הָעוֹלָם,

הַמּוֹצִיא לֶחֶם מִן הָאָרֶץ.

Baruch atah adonai eloheinu melech haolam hamotzi lechem min ha'aretz.

Thank you, God, for the blessing of bread, and for the festive meal which we will now enjoy together.

USHPIZIN

We welcome our holy guests, Abraham, Isaac, Jacob, Joseph, Moses, David, and Aaron. As we recall their lives and good deeds, we remember the generations of Jewish men and women who lived before us.

BIRKAT HAMAZON

BLESSING AFTER THE MEAL

We join in giving thanks for the festive meal we have eaten.

בָּרוּךְ אַתָּה יְיָ, הַזָּן אֶת הַכֹּל.

Baruch atah adonai eloheinu melech haolam hazan et hakol.

עֹשֶׂה שָׁלוֹם בִּמְרוֹמָיו, הוּא יַעֲשֶׂה שָׁלוֹם עָלֵינוּ וְעַל כָּל יִשְׂרָאֵל. וְאִמְרוּ אָמֵן.

Oseh shalom bimromov hu ya'aseh shalom aleinu v'al kol Yisrael v'imru amen.

Thank you, God,
for the festive meal we have shared,
for the harvest we have eaten at this table,
for the Torah and mitzvot which guide our lives,
for Israel, the homeland of the Jewish people,
for our freedom to live as Jews,
for life, strength, and health.
Bless our family, and grant us peace.

BLESSING OVER THE LULAV AND ETROG

Each morning during Sukkot, except for Shabbat, we recite a blessing over the lulav and etrog. We hold the lulav in our right hand and the etrog in our left hand. The stem of the etrog should be pointing up, and the lulav and etrog should be touching.

בָּרוּךְ אַתָּה יְיָ, אֱלֹהֵינוּ מֶלֶךְ הָעוֹלָם,

אֲשֶׁר קִדְּשָׁנוּ בְּמִצְוֹתָיו, וְצִוָּנוּ עַל נְטִילַת לוּלָב.

Baruch atah adonai eloheinu melech ha'olam asher kideshanu b'mitzvotav v'tzivanu al n'tilat lulav.

Thank you, God, for these beautiful and fragrant fruits of the harvest, for the sun and the rain which make them grow, for the seasons of nature and the seasons of our lives.

After we say the blessing, we turn the etrog so that its stem is pointing down, and we wave the lulav and etrog together in all directions.

LIGHTING THE CANDLES

Freely adapted after a version by A.W. BINDER

Freely, as a chant

Ba - ruch a - tah a - do nai e - lo - hei - nu me - lech ha - o - lam, a - sher kid - sha - nu b'mitz - vo - tav v - tzi - va - nu l' - had - lik ner, l' had - lik ner, shel Yom - tov.

SHEHECHEYANU

Traditional

Ba - ruch a - tah a - do nai e - lo - hei - nu me - lech ha - o - lam she - he - che - ya - nu v' - kiy' - ma - nu v' - hi - gi - ya - nu la - z'man ha - zeh.

LESHEV BASUKKAH

TRADITIONAL

Ba - ruch a - tah a - do - nai e - lo - hei - nu me - lech hao - lam a - sher kid - sha - nu b' - mitz - vo - tav v' - tzi - va - nu le - shev ba - suk - kah.

KIDDUSH

TRADITIONAL

Ba-ruch a-tah a-do-nai e-lo-hei-nu me-lech ha-o-lam bo-rei p'-ri ha-ga-fen. A-men. Ba-ruch a-tah a-do-nai e-lo-hei-nu me-lech ha-o-lam a-sher ba-char ba-nu mi-kol am v'-ro-m'-ma-nu mi-kol la-shon v'-kid'-sha-nu b'-mitz-vo-tav. Va-ti-ten la-nu a-do-nai e-lo-hei-nu b'a-ha-vah mo-a-dim l'-sim-cha cha-gim u-z'ma-nim l'-sa-son. Et yom chag ha-suk-kot ha-zeh ze'-man sim-cha te-nu mik-rah ko-desh ze-cher li-tzi-at mitz-ra-yim. ki va-nu va-char-ta v'-o-ta-nu ki-dash-ta mi kol ha-a-mim u-mo-a-dei kod-sh'-cha b'-sim-cha uv'-sa-son hin-chal-ta-nu. Ba-ruch a-tah a-do-nai m'-ka-desh yis-ra-el v' ha-z'ma-nim.

BIRKAT HAMAZON

M. NATHANSON

Flowing, in a thankful manner

Ba - ruch a - tah _____ a - do - nai e - lo - hei - nu me - lech ha - o - lam ha - zan et ha - o - lam ku - lo b'- tu - vo b'- chen b'- che - sed uv' ra - cha - mim hu no - ten le - chem l' chol ba - sar ki l' - o - lam chas - do uv' - tu - vo ha - ga - dol ta - mid lo cha - sar la - nu v' - al yech - sar la - nu ma - zon l' - o - lam va - ed ba - a - vur sh'- mo ha - ga - dol _____ ki hu el zan um' - far - nes la - kol u - mei - tiv la - kol u - mei - chin ma - zon l' - chol b'ri - o - tav a - sher _____ ba - ra. Ba - ruch a - tah _____ a - do - nai _____ ha - zan _____ et ha - kol.

OSEH SHALOM

By N. HIRSH

O - seh shalom bim-ro-mav hu ya'-a-seh shalom a-lei-nu
v'- al kol yis-ra-el v'-im-ru, im-ru a-men. O-ru a-men
Ya-a-seh shalom Ya-a-seh shalom shalom a-lei-nu v'- al kol yis-ra-el
Ya-a-seh shalom Ya-a-seh shalom shalom a-lei-nu v'- al kol yis-ra-el
ya-a-seh shalom ya-a-seh shalom shalom a-lei-nu v'- al kol yis-ra-el
ya-a-seh shalom ya-a-seh shalom shalom a-lei-nu v'- al kol yis-ra-el
ya-a-seh shalom ya-a-seh shalom shalom a-lei-nu v'- al kol yis-ra-el.

©copyright by the author. All rights reserved.

MAYIM

E. AMIRAN

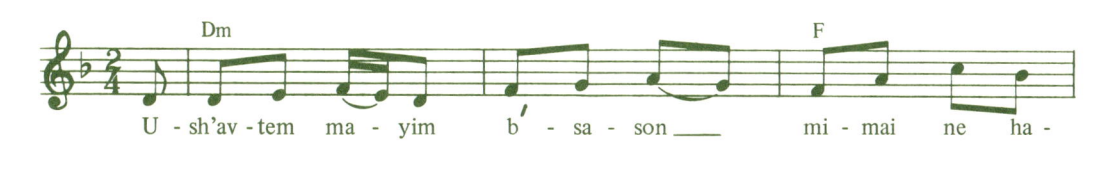

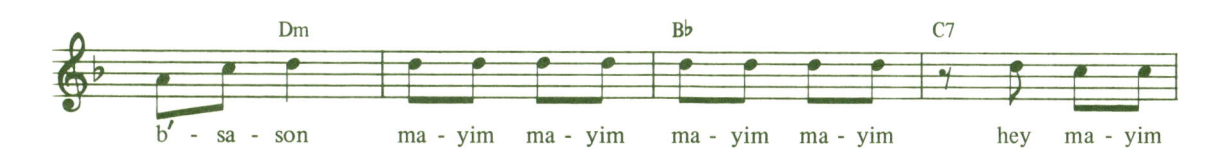

U - sh'av-tem ma - yim b' - sa - son ___ mi - mai ne ha - y' - shu - a u - sh'av-tem ma - yim b' - sa - son ___ mi - mai - ne ha - y' - shu - a ma - yim ma - yim ma - yim ma - yim hey ma - yim b' - sa - son ma - yim ma - yim ma - yim ma - yim hey ma - yim b' - sa - son hey hey hey hey ma - yim ma - yim ma - yim ma - yim ma - yim ma - yim b' - sa - son ma - yim ma - yim ma - yim ma - yim ma - yim ma - yim b' - sa - son.

LAMA SUKKAH ZU?

CHASIDIC MELODY

La - mah suk - kah zu, A - ba tov she - li? li. Le - shev ba - suk - kah ya - ki - ri, Le - shev ba - suk - kah cha - vi - vi, Le - shev ba - suk - kah ye - led chen - ye - led chen she - li.

2. Lamah leshev bah, aba tov sheli?
   Avotenu yakiri,
   Avotenu chavivi,
   Avotenu af gam hemah
   Yashvu basukkah.

VESAMACHTA

FOLK

Ve - sa - mach - ta be - cha - ge - cha ve - ha - yi - ta ach sa - me - ach ach - ach - ach sa - me - ach ach.
Ve - sa - mach - ta be - cha - ge - cha ve - ha - yi - ta ach sa - me - ach ach - ach - sa - me - ach ach.

I'M BUILDING A SUKKAH

FOLK

I'm build-ing a suk-kah. My ham-mer doesn-'t stop. La-di-da bim bam bi-ri bi-ri bam Oh bring me the schach for I've reached the ve-ry top! La-di-da bim bam bi-ri bi-ri bam, La-di-da bim bam bi-ri bi-ri bam.

2. I'll sit in the Sukkah like Noah in the Ark.
   La-di-da, . . .
   I'll drink and be merry from morning to dark!
   La-di-da, . . .

3. Come friends and neighbors, come right along.
   La-di-da, . . .
   Join us in eating and singing a song.
   La-di-da. . . .

Add your own verses!

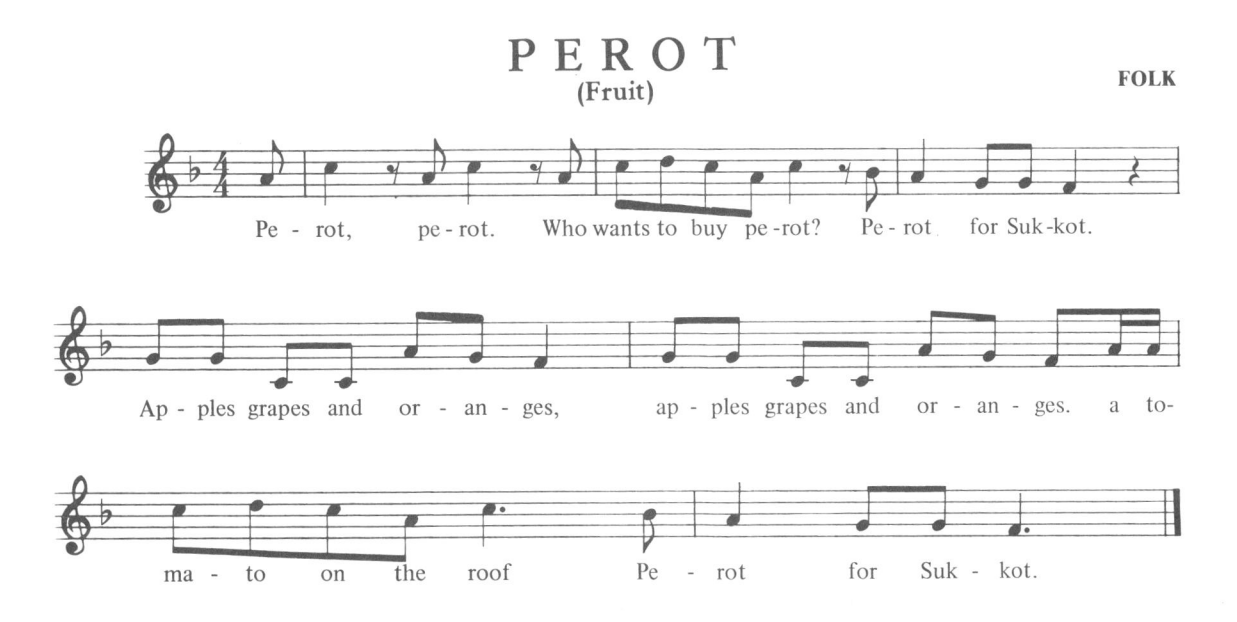

PEROT
(Fruit)

FOLK

Pe-rot, pe-rot. Who wants to buy pe-rot? Pe-rot for Suk-kot. Ap-ples grapes and or-an-ges, ap-ples grapes and or-an-ges. a to-ma-to on the roof Pe-rot for Suk-kot.

Perot, perot.
Mi rotzeh liknot.
Perot lechag Sukkot.
Anavim vetapuchim (2)
Ve'agvaniah
Lit lot al gag sukkah.

37

BUILDING A SUKKAH

Building a sukkah is a mitzvah. It is a custom to hammer the first nail as soon as Yom Kippur is over.

There are only a few rules to follow in building a sukkah, so you can use your imagination.

- A sukkah must be more than two walls, and one of them can be the side of a house, garage, or fence.
- It must be at least three feet high and no more than 30 feet high.
- The walls may be any material — wood, cloth, glass, window shades, chicken wire, or packing crates.
- But the roof — or "schach" — must be made of things that grow: leaves, straw, branches, or cornstalks.
- The sukkah must be more shady than sunny inside.
- The stars must be visible through the roof.

For easy "architectural" plans, see The First Jewish Catalog, Siegel, Strassfeld, and Strassfeld (Jewish Publication Society, 1973); or the Fall 1979 issue of Jewish Living. There are pre-fab sukkot available through Jewish book and gift shops, and Jewish youth groups in many communities have home sukkah-building crews!

DECORATING THE SUKKAH

Even though the sukkah is our home for only one week, we try to make it as beautiful as we can. Some people decorate their sukkah with the seven crops the Jewish people found when they reached the land of Israel. These are: wheat, barley, vines, figs, pomegranates, olives, and honey.

Here are other things that may be used to decorate a sukkah:

Fruits and vegetables
Leaves and branches
Cornstalks
Flowers
Indian Corn
Gourds
Paper lanterns and birds
Original artwork
Popcorn and peanuts
Paper chains
Rosh Hashanah greeting cards
Embroidered cloths
Posters with the Sukkot blessings and names of the "ushpizin"
Pictures of Israel

To protect your paper decorations from the wind and rain, cover them with clear plastic.

If you don't have a sukkah at home, a small one made from a shoe-box makes a lovely centerpiece for holiday meals.

KAR-BEN COPIES PUBLICATIONS

My Very Own Rosh Hashanah
My Very Own Yom Kippur
My Very Own Sukkot
My Very Own Simchat Torah
My Very Own Chanukah
My Very Own Megillah
My Very Own Haggadah
My Very Own Shavuot
My Very Own Jewish Calendar
Come, Let Us Welcome Shabbat
> *by Judyth R. Saypol and Madeline Wikler*

Let's Celebrate — 57 Holiday Crafts
Let's Have A Party
> *by Ruth Esrig Brinn*

Only Nine Chairs — A Tall Tale
Poppy Seeds, Too — A Twisted Tale
> *by Deborah Miller and Karen Ostrove*

The Mouse in the Matzah Factory
> *by Francine Medoff and David Goldstein*

The Children We Remember
> *by Chana Byers Abells*

My Very Own Jewish Home
> *by Andrew Goldstein and Madeline Wikler*

Holiday Adventures of Achbar
> *by Barbara Sofer and Nina Gaelen*

Mi Ani — Who Am I?
> *by Rochelle Sobel and Meir Pluznick*